ON LIFE'S
TERMS

Richard Wanderman, M.D.

Copyright © 2021 by Richard Wanderman, M.D.

All rights reserved. No part of this publication may be reproduced, distributed, or transmitted in any form or by any means, including photocopying, recording, or other electronic or mechanical methods, without the prior written permission of the publisher, except in the case brief quotations embodied in critical reviews and other noncommercial uses permitted by copyright law.

ISBN: 978-1-63945-202-6 (Paperback)
        978-1-63945-201-9 (E-book)

The views expressed in this book are solely those of the author and do not necessarily reflect the views of the publisher, and the publisher hereby disclaims any responsibility for them.

Writers' Branding
1800-608-6550
www.writersbranding.com
orders@writersbranding.com

Contents

A SNOWFLAKE 2
CLOUDS AND IMAGINATION 3
DILEMMAS 4
VIEWS OF LIFE 5
SHILOH 6
REASON FOR BEING 7
PUZZLE FOR THE MIND 9
CHOICES IN LIFE 10
GOALS 11
HEALING THE SOUL 12
NIGHTS 13
THE COLORS OF LIFE 14
TODAY I AM 15
QUESTIONS 16
NATURE AND MIND 17
LIFE'S FEELINGS 18
ATTEND! 19
TODAY'S PROMISES 20
A FIST 21
FANTASY 22
HEROES 23
HEROES 2 24
IMAGES 25
THE RIPPLE EFFECT 26
WHERE DOES INDIVIDUALITY FIT IN? 27
WHO AM I? 28
A NEW DAY 29
DRIFTING 30
RENEWAL OF LIFE 31
INVISIBILITY 32

SUCCESS	34
A BOTTLE	35
THE TASK	36
WHAT IS IMMORTALITY	37
WHY IS IT THAT THE WORLD IS?	38
PENETRATING TRUTH	39
TRUTH'S STRENGTH	40
YOUR CHOICE	41
AGING	42
MIND GAMES	43
LIFE FROM WITHIN	44
SUCCESS MEASURED	45
LIVING	46
POTENTIAL	47
LIVING TAPESTRY	48
FINALITY	49
IS THIS HUMANITY?	50
QUESTIONS OF US	52
AWASH	53
BEING OURSELVES	56
OPTIONS	57
SONGS OF LIFE	58
GROWTH IN PERSPECTIVE	59
CAN REALITY BE TOUCHED?	61
WHERE ARE WE?	62
HOW I SEE IT?	63
THE COMMITTEE OF THEY	65
LIVING WITHIN OURSELVES	66
CHOICES FOR LIFE	68
SILENT STREAMS	70
DAILY ROUTINE	72
DECISIONS ARE CROSSROADS	73
THROUGH YOUNGER EYES	74

LIVING IN DREAMS	75
WHEN ARE WE?	76
EMOTIONALITY	77
EMOTIONS	78
HOW WE LIVE	79
LIFE	81
LIVING 2	82
PRAYER	83
FREE ASSOCIATION	84
GROWTH OF CONVICTION	85
ARE WE THERE YET?	86
SILENCE, PERHAPS	87
TRAVELLER'S LAMENT	89
LIFE'S CLOUDS	90
HOW WE BECOME WHO WE ARE	92
SAGE OR SENIOR	94
TODAY'S CHAOS	96
EXPEDIENCY OR RESPONSIBILITY	97
IMMORTALITY	99
MOULD OR NOT	100

To my children:

Adam, Meredith, Seth, Richard Jr., and Greg.

A SNOWFLAKE

Silver gray flakes fall from the sky
Landing on the window-pane
Exhibiting intricate patterns
Formed from Nature's mind,
Then turning pale and clear
Pulling in upon themselves
And dripping down the pane.

Life's gift to each of us is a snowflake.
We are that flake
Neither more perfect nor immortal
But each an individual
Unique within our shape.

Oct. 20, 1991

CLOUDS AND IMAGINATION

Endless parades of shapes and forms
Passing by in review for us to enjoy.
Different eyes see associations anew
Forming and changing as is the view.

They cheer us or tear us
But never steer us
In the wrong direction.
Only the dark secrets of our mind
Can do this.
And still they float by like flowing water
With no specific form
But that found within our mind.

Balloons without strings
Shapes without forms
Masses without solidity
Imaginings without end.
Pushed, unrushed by unseen hands,
Evidence of forces not felt by the senses
Forming and changing
As endlessly as is our imagination.

July 31, 1992

DILEMMAS

Life is full of dilemmas,
The food of growth.
We can choose
To grow or die.
To face them and live
To hide, and die.

July 3, 1994

VIEWS OF LIFE

As we sit, shop and play
We let our subconscious roam.
It soars, seeks answers
To questions never spoken,
For it lives in a world
Beyond our view
Directing us in what to do.

Let us fly above the sky
Looking back on our life.
What we see may be what we get
What we had, or what may be,
For our free will can change all that.

Tomorrow's flames are fanned by today's winds
Forcing glowing embers to ignite
Highlighting what's within our view
By coloring how we see,
With desire, fear or pleasantry

But deep within our being,
The truth lurks,
Sending forth darts to align our thoughts
With knowledge of what can be.
How we change and how we may grow
Is all that life will let us know.

July 3, 1994

SHILOH

Seeing stars turn on at night,
Sensing the air mysteriously stir
Awakens the inner soul
Introducing a new sense of order.

Walking on ground anointed by blood
Hearing voices on the wind,
Feeling the presence of souls,
Knowing the strong emotions
Of love's lost and dreams unfulfilled,
Settles upon us to search our soul.

Sharing the peaches of yesterday's tears
And holding, loving, bonding
Where anguish, pain, sorrow, despair
Have dedicated this ground,
Announcing and defining the cycle of life.
Seeing the sun set, the moon rise
Reminds me of these past lives
The ones that were here and now long gone
As we tread these grounds and pass along.

July 16, 1994

REASON FOR BEING

Staring through this open window
Seeing a world of blue skies, billowy white/grey clouds
And multicolored trees swaying with an invisible breeze.
Thinking of life and love with emotions that bathe me
In yesterday's smiles and tomorrow's sighs,
Filling my mind with images and enchanted daydreams,
But always drawing me back to today's realities.

How far need we travel from home
To find security within ourselves?
Only as far as the nearest room within our mind,
Which affords us space to think and feel without
Being influenced by those around us.
Thus, we carry our own escape within us.

But when and how do we find the time to travel this path?
Where do we need to be to enter our sanctuary?
Why is it so complicated?
We need only to find our reason for being
For the fuel to fire our quest,
And lose ourselves within ourselves
And divorce the need for the when, the how, or the why,
And drift into the relaxation of our senses.

We then drink of our soul and learn to endure
The demands of our lives that chip away at our defenses.
For our problems do not disappear like a vapor,
Nor are they magically resolved as in fairy tales,
But their pressing nature subsides
And the options for their solution form
To be objectively evaluated.

Thus in the midst of our troubled sea of pain
We need but to rely upon ourselves to avoid the drain.

July 4, 1994

PUZZLE FOR THE MIND

Towering above
Reflects cowering below.
As ins become outs
And yeses, noes.
Yet as we are here
We can still be there.
Climbing above
Only to find we are below.
Seemingly here now
We are recognized then.
Therefore we get to after
For after proceeds before.
But since then can be now
We really are here
While still being there.

Sept. 1, 1994

CHOICES IN LIFE

Visions float in and out of our consciousness
Reminding us of past experiences and future desires.
Each has its emotional value,
A price tag exacted from our being.
Some bring soothing thoughts
To relax our tensed muscles,
Others promote anxiety or simply unpleasantry
No matter which form it takes
We have a choice of our reaction,
Sad, happy, upset, angry,
Frustration can give way to serenity.
Find the positive which is ever present,
And choose to see it, as it is meant.

Sept. 1, 1994

GOALS

As time passes, situations change
But our goals need remain the same.
We can modify the path but not the end,
Our lives are in a continual flux.
Frustration is often, and discontent develops
As signals form our subconscious
To test our resolve and commitment,
A sign we have lost our way.
Frustration acknowledges our avoidance
Of necessary steps.
Discontent acknowledges a situation blocking
Our forward progress.
Neither may be necessary, most are temporary.
Focus upon the positive, dwell on the pleasantries of life.
Relegate the negative to be temporarily endured
And work toward our goals.
The future is ours to grasp and hold tight.
The present is but a passing phase,
A stepping stone.
The past is our guide.
So set our goals, then reset new ones,
And the future is ours.

Sept. 30, 1994

HEALING THE SOUL

Sparkling lights
Dance before my eyes as I lay down
To ponder the days events,
Glowing, lighting the night sky above my head
Soothing the thoughts, exploding upon my mind
Bringing me to realize the timelessness of time
Set there by a loving hand to delight the soul
And to heal the mental wounds of the day.

Oct. 1, 1994

NIGHTS

Single lights fill the sky with flares of sonorous silence
Illuminating our hearts and betraying our age.
Single lights fill the sky with points of anonymity
Remembering our bygone days and enhancing our dreams.
Single lights fill the sky with shades of blind obscurity
Emphasizing our mortality and observing our destiny.
To know them
Is to know the past.
To see them
Is to see the passage of time.

Oct. 27, 1994

THE COLORS OF LIFE

A flow of brown highlighting a pale pink
Focusing upon green pools floating above a red lake.

Tones of vibrant sounds
Drift across timeless space
Punctuating nature's talent
To harness harmony.

Movement disturbs the air
Bringing attention to itself
Gracefully and purposely
Dressed in serenity.

Flights of fright forage for finality
But pacific pauses produce peace.

Browns, pink, green and red harness the harmony
Of graceful movement foraging for an inner peace.

April 17, 1995

TODAY I AM

Today I am
For it is my day.
Tomorrow I'll be
For it is there.
The next day
I'll go on.

Celebrate
Today
As a special
Day.
Live
Today
For it is
Yours.

April 17, 1995

QUESTIONS

Answers to unspoken questions
Float upon unseen currents
Falling upon unhearing ears.
Striding forward
Headlong into unknown quests
Trying to resolve unheralded events.

Simple math does not simply add units.
Fractions occur to disrupt the laminar flow
And rebuild a semisolid base.

People are never simple.
Slight gestures or words
Can bring tears or smiles.
No thought need be present,
Only the confluence of sounds.

April 17, 1995

NATURE AND MIND

Beneath grey skies, green trees grow
Feeding on the life giving moisture
Shared by the clouds.
Above the grey lining, blue skies reign
Giving life sustaining light
To the greenery below.

Man walks among the trees, looking to the sky
Seeing the grey vault
And wondering why he is overcast.
Then within him, his mind soars
Flying beyond the visual limits
And traveling to unimagined heights.

Grey skies and the sun's light nourish the trees
Man's mind nourishes his soul.

April 30, 1995

LIFE'S FEELINGS

Life's feelings, an ebb and flow,
Questioning needs and desires.
Mountains to be climbed,
Fields easily trod,
Walls to daunt the staunchest.

Life's style changes with the seasons
Once appropriate may fall to another
Though all dance through our dreams
Tethered to our souls as slip knots
To be drawn tighter or released.

Commitment looms above the open plains
Casting its shadow, causing chills.
Winds howl across desert dunes
Unchecked by grains of sand
But repelled by the cliffs of change.

We stand confused upon this path
Daring to scale, but content upon the lea.
Silently scenes scroll across our mind's eye.
Pasts are idolized, people once cherished,
A tug of war upon the soul.

May 4, 1995

ATTEND!

Attend
Stand firm
Attend.
Raised arms
Fisting the air
Attend.
Move forward
Attend.
Purposeful strides
Trampling delicate ground
Attend.
Take charge
Attend.
Encircle the goal
Enfold the arms
Attend—attend.

June 14, 1995

TODAY'S PROMISES

A hand descends upon the stillness
Confounding the darkness,
Stirring vibrant colors swirling to mix
And creating a shout
Heard only by the vigilant
Contemplating their inner soul,
Equally aware of their infirmities
As of life's inequities

Carets dangled before veiled eyes
Blinded by the promises of future finds
Surreptitiously lose sight of
Current events in order to pursue
Avenues of imaginary plentitude,
And fail to grasp the significance
Of today's offerings.

Silken robes wrap designed bodies
Barely hiding overt secrets
Of hoped to be assets,
Totally missing the basic value of
Nature's hand in her aesthetic application
Of natural choices and basic instincts
All that's worthy of sincere appreciation
Reflects nature's hand in its creation.
The rest is but a reflection
Cast from shadows of
A promise of unfathomable deception.

July 25,1995

A FIST

A hand
Closed in a
Fist
Not for Fighting
But to offer
Strength.

Dec. 31, 1995

FANTASY

Fantasy
Embraces us all
Even those
Who deny it
Causing
Dreams
To become
Reality

Dec. 31, 1995

HEROES

Yesterday's heroes
Awaken
Forgotten loves
Of fearsome foes
And fearless
Friends.

Dec. 31, 1995

HEROES 2

Fanfare
For returning
Heroes
Unfold
The flag
For Freedom

Dec. 31, 1995

IMAGES

Passing clouds
Draw
Innumerable images
Causing
The mind's eye
To awaken

Dec. 31, 1995

THE RIPPLE EFFECT

Events
Unknown to us
Ripple
Upon
Our minds
And
Influence
Our lives.

Dec. 21, 1995

WHERE DOES INDIVIDUALITY FIT IN?

Ringing
Alters one's cognition
Bringing a renewed
Awareness.

Stillness
Reflects thought;
Noise
Represents deed;
Existence
Lives in sound.

Single days pass
Challenging time,
Racing on future's
Path.

So where
Does
Individuality
Fit in?

March 8, 1996

WHO AM I?

Awakening to raucous
Sounds
Bringing awareness
Of life's
Existence.
Time defines
Our lives.
But who
Am I?

March 8, 1996

A NEW DAY

Fast approaching comes a new day
Filled with wonder and mystery
Soon to be heard from and openly seen
With sound and forms yet to be guessed at.
It has a soft touch,
Caressing and warm,
Accepting and trusting,
Giving without cause
Expecting without thought.
The world continues its growth,
Questions are always asked,
Answers echo within its halls.
Life is renewed.

March 4, 1998

DRIFTING

Sailing through the seas of time
Destined to wander without direction
To be gathered in the lines of fate's cast-offs
Churning, seeking but lost without direction.

Firmly set upon the deck,
Swaying in nonexistent breezes
To tunes heard within deafened ears
Visually seeking that which is hidden
Behind curtains of thickened air.

Reaching with outstretched arms
Frustrated by absent hands
Yearning to know, feel, see, hear
But destined to forever chase a dream
Of goals not yet defined.

March 4, 1998

RENEWAL OF LIFE

Fast approaching a new day
Filled with wonder and mystery.
Soon to be heard and seen,
Sounds and forms only guessed at.
The soft touch
Caressing and warm,
Accepting and trusting,
Given without cause,
Expected without thought.
The world continues to grow
Questions always asked but
No answers echo within the halls,
Life has been renewed.

March 4, 1998

INVISIBILITY

Invisibility stands before you
Shedding its mortal form
Taking on the shapes of shadows of
People milling about whose names you know
But few taking form with firm outlines.
Instead, ahead lies a durable darkness
Shrouding the light within their eyes
Sending out rays only to be echoed
By enclosing night.

Silently we walk among the shadows
Cast upon the air,
Animated and solid
But unresponsive there.

Take care lest the songs of silence
Ringing within your ears,
Rob you of sight and sound,
Stabbing through seams in the darkness,
Parting the gossamer veils
To seek other silent silhouettes.

Laughter forces a wedge within this vice
Caring not for supposed form
But carried on wings of innocence
To explode this intricate network
Of veiled fences surrounding people,
By opening their eyes
And allowing a spark of light
To illuminate their scene,
But just as fast gone
To seek shelter
Among more exuberant hosts.

Jan. 9, 1999

SUCCESS

Success
Flies us forward;
A lantern
Lights our feet.

Her face
Enlivened by
Her smile;
A rose
Yearns
For the sun.

Jan. 9, 1999

A BOTTLE

Gray waters hurry by
Carrying the world from north to south.
A bottle cast into its placid flow
Reflects the change of the land
And man's egocentric hand.
It drifts from one ideology to another
Each so sure of its truth
That it tries to exclude the other.
But our bottle drifts on
Unrepentant of its non-alignment
Reflecting back man in his glory
So he can see what he wants to see.
Passing thousands of years as it travels
Equally unmoved by blight and blessing
Serene within itself
Until it washes ashore.

Feb. 19, 1999

THE TASK

What makes us feel that what is simple
Should not be?
Guilt over a task's simplicity
Is more pain than complicity.

Go forth with your tool
Release the air from your chest,
Beat the bushes of your talent
But cry not at the rest.

We're told by folks of olde
That only good comes from the sweat of our brow
Fear not what moves you
Even if it be simple now.

Feb. 19, 1999

WHAT IS IMMORTALITY

What is immortality?
To live beyond our usefulness
Just to please either our ego
Or the needs of others?
Or perhaps to maintain our youth and
Vitality through bioengineered devises
Made to look natural, but really
To replace worn out flesh?
Or maybe it lies within our essence
To travel through time and space
To make ourselves felt
From some ethereal plane?
Or could it be a memory
Relayed from one to another
Instilled as the essence of ourselves
And bottled as Love?
You pick,
But pick wisely.

Feb. 19, 1999

WHY IS IT THAT THE WORLD IS?

Why is it that the world is?
A plane can fly from point to point
And theoretically never move;
A ray of sun can illuminate and warm
But its speed never varies;
The sounds of night reverberate
But are never so loud during the day;
Hard upon the heels of a wind
A storm blows itself away;
We travel beyond know space
Yet the sky only minutely changes;
Our minds create our world
And are still a mystery;
Why is it that the world is?

Steam seeps through crevices,
And roots
Split rocks.

Heat reflects light,
An oasis
May really be.

Deserts are alive,
Yet sand
Is inert.

Castaway your doubts,
We are
Here!

April 7, 1999

PENETRATING TRUTH

Strength of the soul
Strength of the light
Penetrates even our
Darkest night.
The mind closes
The mind denies
But strength
Penetrates even our
Darkest lies.
Knowing the truth
Knowing the way
Penetrates even our
Darkest day.
Silence of the night
Silence of our way
Penetrates even our
Darkest bray.
The truth is
As the truth does
And each of us
Stands before it
Naked.

April 13, 1999

TRUTH'S STRENGTH

Strength of the soul
Strength of the light
Penetrates even our
Darkest night.
The mind closes down
The mind denies
But light
Penetrates even our
Darkest lies.
Knowing the truth
Knowing the way
The answers
Illuminate our
Darkest day.
Silence of the night
Silence of our way
Dampens even our
Loudest bray.
The truth is
As the truth does
For each of us
Stand before it naked.

April 13, 1999

YOUR CHOICE

Sandal-footed strolling past the gates of light
To emerge upon a plane beyond our sight.
Standing alone
While all about me shimmers and shines
Helps to remind me of pasts' long ago times.
Before me is the warp and weave
Stretching its hands to grasp our thoughts.
Stunned, amazed that can be seen,
This scene from a surrealist's brush.
But wait,
Arrest that hand,
Where am I going and into what land?
We all,
Each of us can be
Whatever we want to make of we.
With this about me and in my head
I know, beyond a doubt, which way to go about.
So those of you who still do not hear
Be wise, be kind and lend an ear,
A way is provided, provide you know
How much you want what it is you sow.

April 13, 1999

AGING

Shriveled crops slumber
Their age soon to end,
Drying in eternal heat while
Basking in summer's earthy pasture.
Once young and strong,
Giving nurture to man from nature
Flowering, reaching for the sun
Bring forth the beauty and plentitude
For which it was meant.
But now
Past its prime, drying and dieing
Turning back to earth tones
Once again to reunite with the soil
And become the nourishment
For future toil.

Jan. 12, 2010
March 1, 2000

MIND GAMES

Reports come in detailing events
Currently unfolding
Filling our consciousness with images
Of foreign sites and causes
Evoking sensations
Unwittingly drawn out by subconscious
Fears and implanted prejudices.
Opinions, nothing more!
But how they control our world!
Facts are in the hands of the believer.
Facts are laid upon the stage of life
For all to see and each to hold.
Facts are seen as they are wished
To be seen, by you, by me.
The truth of a tale is in the telling.
As long as it fits into our vision,
As long as it fulfills our belief,
It is true.
We are all different.
Therefore, so is our sight.

April 2002

LIFE FROM WITHIN

Alone in a room full of ghosts
Who appear to us as angels
Robed in flowing gowns
But without faces.
Silent shouts pierce my head
Causing me to wince and frown,
And float within my soul as a cloud of
Dispersing sparks,
Shredding me,
Shooting pains through me, and
Laughing.

We are sliding down a slanting slope
Riding sleighs gathering speed
To burst forth
And raise our faces,
Marshal our forces
And let loose a cry of anguish.
For we are but a shade upon our land
But if we open our minds
We may leave our image.

Sept. 13, 2002

SUCCESS MEASURED

Success is measured in many ways,
Each is within the eye of the beholder
Or upon the mind of the molder.
Society is oft the ruler of success
Granting status to the obvious.
Financial reward usually follows
And is used to judge the unknown.
Personal knowledge becomes cardinal
When the external obscures the internal.
History crowns those with the best publicity
But only you and I know for ourselves.
Only from within can we know the truth.
Which of us are really successful?
Only we can follow the signs
Left to light the path to our goals.
Success is fleeting.
If once reached, it defines us.
So what is success?
To each his own.

Oct. 2002

LIVING

Wings wide
Yearning to feel the freedom of flight.
Muscles straining
To soar above the chords of time,
Continually passing
Through realms of dreams and deeds
Recording fantasies of a people's myths
Being used as tenets of truth.
The senses flow
Intermingling with life's clothes,
Covering scenes of mundane moods.
Where are we within this continuum?
Asleep or awake?
Alive or in limbo?

Dec. 2002

POTENTIAL

Holes etched on the blackness of time
Describe patterns of yesteryears and
Reflect interpretations of tomorrow.
Revolving within our subconscious are
Games played out over the years
To illuminate our darknesses.

Relationships plagued within our emotions
Dance before our mind's eye and
Draw our thoughts along familiar patterns,
To ruts of mental servitude and depression.
Stretching and eager to escape the dungeons
Of our own making we turn to the familiar
And desperately cling to the known
Waiting for our time to come forth and burst free,
To fly before the convention, to elude expectation
And to redefine ourselves
To be what we can be,
Not what "they" determine for us to be.
Those faint of heart, fail.
But those of stronger fiber
Unfold their wings and Soar.

June 22, 2003

LIVING TAPESTRY

Connections are severed and formed daily
Taking from us and adding to us threads
That weaves the tapestry of our lives.
Forever changing themes flow in and out,
Opening and closing selected doors,
Seemingly at random—
The portals to within ourselves.
But, to where do they lead?
Into what tapestry do they intrude?
Pondering such complexities leads us
To a dizzying spiral of inanities.
The interweaving threads determines for us
Where we offer our interwoven patterns
As they are incorporated within the tapestry
Of the present.
Our lives are not perfection,
There are flaws within the patterns,
But not to weave is not to live
And not to live opens a hole,
An entry that may unravel the whole.

May 10, 2004

FINALITY

Standing still,
Reflecting.
The mind sings songs
Never heard nor conceived,
Sliding down corridors ever narrowing
And spacious beyond being.
Thoughts echo about folded planes
Traveling along limitless horizons,
Delving into hidden crevices
Meant to be unknown.
Silence expands upon the echoes
Reverberating from the sounds
Which shields it
Form fields of rainbows.
A final tear falls
Then silence regains
Its throne.

Nov. 22, 2004

IS THIS HUMANITY?

A hand reaches out
Grasping for anything
But is clasped by emptiness.

A mind cries out
Feeling for anyone
But is received by none.

A soul stretches out
Hungering for another
But is chilled by the void.

Gone!
Where are they?
Can this be reality
Or is this but a reflection
Of our modern facade?

Emptiness has filled our beings
Replacing society's hold
Redefining our goals
Refurbishing our souls.

Terror dominates our news
Reporters commoners, innocents
Are sacrificed to gain attention.
Murderers become heroes.

Where is the outrage?
Politicians, leaders, and readers
Discuss the situation.
But where is their heart?

This is not the norm!
We may be distracted,
Even distanced
But we are human!
Aren't we?

Nov. 22, 2004

QUESTIONS OF US

I sit here in wonder
Staring at the snow blanketed scene
Feeling the still chill in the air
Asking no one in particular
Where I am in this picturesque world,
Who am I supposed to be and why am I here.
No answer comes.
No glimmer of light.
No ray of sunshine.
Nothing,
But the scene is beautiful.
Why do we expect answers?
We already know the where, who, and why.
Our conceit is enormous
But our need is greater.
We surround ourselves with evidences,
We collect tomes of convoluted proof
But we do not believe, we are paralyzed.
Look!
The answer is before our eyes.

Dec. 23, 2004

AWASH

Awash in a sea of serenity
Aware of the tides of solitude,
The ebb and flow of time
Bathing the barren beaches of reflection.

Standing among the towering titans,
Basking in their every word,
Drinking in the pearls they cast,
And gathering them into strands of wisdom.

We kneel before the alter
Of senseless visions
Broadcast by myopic priests
Of the masses seeking to sell time
Or place
Or thing.

Awash in this world of chaos
Aware of only our needs,
The ebb and flow of meaningless words
Bathing our eager ego.

But there,
There in their midst,
Rising above the mass of confusion,
A calm head
With placid features
Scans the turbulent throng
Smiles,
Just smiles.
What does he know?
His secret shouts from his face.
He slowly turns to gaze
Upon a few,
A few,
A few who search
With their eyes,
Their hearts,
Their love.

Awash in this sea of tranquility
Aware of the strength of dreams,
The ebb and flow of life,
Bathing in the banners of beauty.

A truth for all to see
A principle for all to hold
A moral for all to know,
Life Is To Be Lived!
Life Is To Be Loved!

In each of us is this being
Reaching to be embraced
Silently scratching at our inner core
Passing notes,
Whispering words,
Humming tunes.

Awash in our sea of silence
Aware of our inner dreams,
The ebb and flow of life,
Bathing our every thought.

March 18, 2005

Comment: We forget where we are going and get caught up in the modern media. We need to come back to who we are.

BEING OURSELVES

Why do we seek to alter ourselves
When we are growing and changing
Becoming the best we can be?
Who is this for?
For you? For me?
This is insane.
We are who we are
None of us can be what another wants
Not even only for a minute.
We are who we are
Developed within,
The character without,
Searching for an answer that does not exist,
Seeking an image portrayed in fantasy.
You, I,
We are who we are
We do not need to change.
I accept you with all your perfection
And you me with all my faults.
Seeing this is to free our energy
To become more of who we are
And to give of what we have:
Our knowledge of life,
Our experience of living,
Our wisdom of error.
Join with me in the search,
Hold my hand for this adventure.
We can dance to our own music,
We can sing with our own voice,
We are who we are:
Alive and vibrant and together.

March 21, 2005

OPTIONS

Upon this road called living,
We stumble into and onto adventures
Which mold our character.
We are taught to deal with these experiences
With rote reactions dictated
By historic precedent.
We are admonished to conform
To society's expectations
And guided by cultural dictates.
But who are we to mindlessly
Practice the norms of yesterday's dictates?
Why do we even consider the options
When we know what is right
And how to act?
Who among us is free enough
To approach this dilemma with
An open mind and unencumbered soul?
To each is given a mind to think,
To each a reason to consider.
Yet we dally over inconsequentials
And permit the truths to elude.
Where are the leaders who lead?
Where are the doers who do?
Look within ourselves as we emerge.

April 29, 2005

SONGS OF LIFE

Silhouetted against the darkening sky
With a halo of red and gold
Reflecting upon an oceans glitter,
Undulating swells oppose receding wells
To fill the air with harmony.
Sailing upon this sea of sound
Tossed and turned by the waves of emotion
Rising and falling within ourselves
As we listen to the songs of our lives.
Breath and tear, controlled by these notes
Flowing through an ethereal plane,
Unite at once the singer and the song.
To be so blessed as to be bathed
By this melodic flow filling our ears
And stirring our hearts, we surreptitiously
Ease into a hidden corner
To be cleansed in the flow of the glow
Of this ocean's tide.
Who is the chanteuse who controls us so?
It is the love in our heart.

Aug. 11, 2005

GROWTH IN PERSPECTIVE

Standing upon the banks of the river
Reviewing my life as others' drift before me,
I pause to contemplate a passing piece of wood
Obviously from a man made structure,
Torn asunder by some natural force,
Sent to relay a message to those willing to receive it
About their mortality and memory.

Apart from our ego, immortality rests within our progeny
Settled to battle the stings of youthful perspective
And the arrows of contemporary opinion.
Within this morass of confused thinking
The twinkle of a lantern, carried furtively,
To illuminate the path so few have taken,
Attempts to direct our steps and pull us forward.
Forward to our chosen destiny.
For we do choose it,
Either by acting or opting not to act
When faced with decisions.

How far we have come from that bundle
Carried in our mother's arms.
Nourished at her breast,
Instructed by her actions,
Encouraged by her love.
Though often pushed from behind or pulled
Kicking into the future.
Feeling unprepared and naked,
But truly clothed in armor fitted
And adjusted by love,
To face life's challenges and
To defeat its vagaries.

Sept. 29, 2006

CAN REALITY BE TOUCHED?

Can reality be touched?
Can one reach out one's hand and feel its shape?
Can one's mind engage it in intercourse
And encompass it with tendrils of thought?

How do we see ourselves?
Can we really know what is within our grasp?
Do we see how we effect others?
Do we really know how we effect ourselves?

We become our own mentors
Guiding our actions with our thoughts
And our thoughts with our actions.
Which comes first?
Which is primary?

How we think directs what we do
So if the results are unacceptable to us
Change what we do thus alter our results
And reinforce our resolve.
Changing our thoughts means changing our actions
For thoughts and actions define our reality.

For as has been said:
Talk is cheap,
Actions speak louder than words.

Nov. 17, 2006

WHERE ARE WE?

Icy strands of silvery light
Reflect from slowly undulating
Currents of crystallized snow.
Motes of dust write their history
Upon the currents of air.
What story do they tell?
Whose life is reflected in their passing?
As we can discern infinitesimal
Scratches on electronic discs,
Why can we not read the images
Passing before our eyes on the
Wings of the wind?

So sure are we in our conceit
Of our powers, we blissfully
Ignore the scripts written upon our environs.
Nature speaks to us through our senses
But we have tuned her out
And allowed our intellect to override our destiny.

Awake to who we are!
Embrace our potential!
Synchronize with our life!

Jan. 31, 2007

HOW I SEE IT?

Visions of aromatic melodies bathe my mind,
Seeping within the crevices of forgetfulness and
The mountains of light.
Deep into thought sings the passion of the senses
Enduring wounds of affectation and slights of frivolity.
Here and there reside way-stations offering
Solace and solitude, with serenity encroaching
Upon the edges of consciousness.

Afloat within the matrix of the mind
A seine of involved artifices embraces me
Enforcing its presence upon my awareness
By creeping onto my creativity.
Alert to the possibility of contamination
I defend myself upon the grounds of self-incrimination
And fend off the incursions aimed at defeating my vision.
Here and now I yet cling to the assumptions
Set down at the beginning of my time,
Put in place by figures bigger than life
But well settled within the realm of reality.
I prevail because of my systems of support
Designed to encourage me to continue
Plunging into the uncharted seas of creativity
With expression unheard of before.

I am me, what I create represents me,
What I do reflects the inner strain to release me,
And it is but a poor excuse for an explanation.
It is untutored and wild, but constrained and directed,
It tells a story which emanates from my soul
And gives back the subject and the thought.
Feeling the melodies drift through my mind,
Define the visions imprinted within my thoughts
Encounter the aromas of memory
And shape my creation.

7/30/07

THE COMMITTEE OF THEY

A standard of societal acceptance defines our moves.
By it, we are all measured.
But from whence does it originate?
Who or what establishes it as the standard?
Why do we kneel at the alter of the Committee of They
As if we were to be knighted because we conform?
Away with this restrictive abuse of our individuality!
We deserve better for our thoughts and deeds.

Standards of interpersonal living are helpful
In allowing us to interact with out trespassing on another's space.
Standards of interpersonal politeness are useful
In permitting us to communicate without giving umbrage.
But standards of societal acceptance serve only to limit
Our individuality and mold us to an arbitrary form
Useful for manipulation, but useless to our personal growth.

7/30/07

LIVING WITHIN OURSELVES

Misty landscapes fly by the window of the mind
Triggering thoughts not visited for years.
Pictures of scenes long since died in life
But still vivid within our eyes.
Memories not bidden but surfacing nonetheless
Engaging our thoughts and directing our gaze.
Thoughts, images imprinted, events no longer viable,
Willfully disrupt our being and usurp our day.
Where do we go as these recriminations
Envelop our thinking?
Where can we hide when we know these things
Are still swimming within our unconscious?
Still, life goes on with its headlong plunge into the future.
Allowing the past to steer,
Even unbeknownst to our waking mind,
Determining our destiny.

Do we allow this to continue and rob us of our will?
Can we not correct our course to confirm today's needs?
Need we delve within our soul to root out our ghosts?

We must take over the tasks and become the masters.
We must grab hold of life and force it,
Virtually choke it, into submission,
Exerting our will and exercising our right
To control our destiny.
Can we, do we, must we do it?
Yes, but only when and if we decide.
Then we must take the appropriate actions.
Then we must persevere
And in the end, we must win.

Dec. 18, 2007

CHOICES FOR LIFE

Strands of time, like a curtain
Covers the vistas of the future
Flowing like lava over the landscapes of tomorrow.
Shimmering in undulating movements while allowing
Glimpses into the march of histories.
Within this cascade of torrential flows,
A single cell floats oblivious to unfolding events
Seeking its own path and its own destiny.
Seeking a place to plant itself where it will be nourished,
Sheltered and encouraged to become all it can be.

Standing alone atop a hill
Gazing forward to the infinite futures,
Seeing possibilities beyond imagination,
Feeding upon the sun's golden rays,
Washing in the currents of time
It moves—taking a slow purposeful step
Directed toward the day's end
Alive with an internal flame
And coated within the cloak of time.

Perhaps we have forgotten him
Lost in our self-centered quest for life,
Crowned with the mantle of selfishness.
We seek, but never find the key.
We ask but never the right questions.
We demand and fall into the traps of war.
All with the idea that we are better,
In fact we are the best,
Not withstanding those who surpass us.

A cell drifts within this milieu of confusion
Steeped in the matrix of society's laws
Defined by its own inimitable ways,
Searching for the path sought by saner minds.
Draped within the strands of time,
Hidden from view by the curtains of prejudice
But still able to peek beyond its limits,
Emitting a plea barely heard by straining ears
Still seeking the route out of the maze.
And arriving decorated with garlands of peace,
Surrounded by jackals of discord,
Draped with jewels of doctrines
And almost smothered with proposals of truth,
It walks steadfastly onward
Ignoring the crowds of seekers
The harbingers of future confusions,
Offering its insight to those wise enough to see
And its voice to those wise enough to hear.

Choices abound to us all
We have but to pick them from the tree of life.
To partake in their feast
We only need to open our hearts and minds
Internalize their truths and the paths to it,
Then to practice our craft and to work.
To expand the effort and enjoy the reward,
A personal paradise for us to live in
And to spread it within the ripples crossing the lands.

Dec. 19, 2007

SILENT STREAMS

Streaking streams of seamless silence
Pour through pores of principles
Laid down by nameless soles
Arrogantly accounting for man's destinies.
Actions define our being
While thoughts define or hearts.
An open hand offers aid as well as asks for alms
But a closed fist denotes trouble.

We stand before the judges of history
Decades after our demise
To be judged and valued by the prejudices
Of our surrogates and biographers.
Where and how do we insert the truths,
Adapting and shaping the circumstances of our time and place
Upon the minds of those who judge us,
So they can enhance their own advantage and hindsight?

It seems in our arrogance we determine our sight.
We who should know better apply these insights
To circumstances more primitive than our experiences
And carry out our judgments with little or no heed to truth.
This becomes a double-edged sword
For after us will come another generation
With its own biases to be applied to ours.

Future thoughts cannot be known
Just as past reasoning is obscure.
Today we are who we are because of who we were.
And tomorrow will come to haunt us for today's values will be gone.
Thus we need only to live in today and worry not of tomorrow,
Seeking our paths through the maze of life's choices
And applying truth as we see and know it.
For the silent streams flow forever.

Dec. 25, 2007

DAILY ROUTINE

I daily enter my car
To transport me to work
To a plane beyond reality.
I travel roads rutted by routine and
Those blazed by creativity.
I enter my office to begin my day
A mundane search for sustenance.
But first, I plan my escape
To worlds yet young in dreams.
The day proceeds, the work, challenging.
I take what is spoken as it is said
And distill it to what needs to be done.
My mind works on and is honed by
Situations seen from new perspectives
Setting the stage for new directions.
Finally the day is over,
The phone calls finished,
The books closed.
It is past, it is done,
But now the real work is begun
To change my dreams into reality.

April 7, 1999

DECISIONS ARE CROSSROADS

There are times in life that take one's breath away
This can be from joy or pain, elation or defeat.
It can fill one's chest with emptiness as a pressure
Waiting to implode.

They are reminders of our humanity and mile markers
Of where we are and how far we have to go.
Heeding these signs allows us to grow and develop
As human beings capable of change as
Our comfort zones are ruptured and can never be the same.
We have a choice of which road to take.
Some will stray into oblivion using chemicals to soften the blows,
To hide—to shrink away from life.
Others will stride forth into the fray to fight through the pain,
To ultimately grasp the ropes of life and live.

The path becomes easier after the initial decision,
But the pain remains as a reminder of our flaws.
We can choose oblivion and escape but only at the huge price of
Never looking back nor inward—never growing—
Deteriorating within ourselves, shrinking from life.
Or we can choose life and enter into the fight to be battered and bruised,
To suffer the stings of perceived misfortune,
But to grow and be given hope and a chance of winning—
Not a gamble—but a real chance of becoming a better person
And to live a life that is fuller and more satisfying.

This is a crossroads, a fork, a divergence.
Two paths, both clouded by the mists of the unknown
Both ready, even eager to help us along
But not with similar results.

Jan. 8, 2008

THROUGH YOUNGER EYES

I see life through younger eyes
Everything seems fresh, new.
The air is alive with dancing lights
The colors glow with radiant beauty.
Sounds echo through unseen chambers
And burst upon my ears
With tingling tones that tickle me.

Age is but a chronological count
It reflects the days during which wisdom accrues.
It is an attitude thrust upon us by society
Trying to strip us of our youth
To pass the mantle of leadership to those less seasoned.
Deep inside we must choose whether or not
To participate in society's dictates
Or to opt out and continue to live.

Yet here I am registered as a senior citizen
Never accepting the cloak of age
And in awe of the wisdom stored
And accessed when needed.
Talking, listening, hearing, and seeing
All through younger eyes.
Evaluating, discerning, understanding, and knowing
With wisdom's experience to guiding me through.
There are advantages to age.

May 15, 2008

LIVING IN DREAMS

Aroused by sibilant sounds
The night's hush hastens our dreams
Wandering beyond the limits
Of casual cares to shores of sensorial sands
Raising thoughts of heightened fears
And scenes of delighted hopes.

This is the world in which we wrap ourselves
Snuggly encased within the cocoon of our making
As we struggle to escape or be secure.
Worlds go by and time passes
We do not notice anything but ourselves
As we blindly soar between mountains of hopes
And oceans of dreams single mindedly setting our sights
On tomorrow's deeds while focusing on today's needs.

Sometimes, in moments of madness, we bend down
To pick up a mote, encased in earthly garb
Which gives off waves of ethereal hints
Begging us to follow our dreams not walk away.
Neither we nor they can hold it for long
But sometimes it seeps into our soul
Causing volcanoes of spontaneous creativity
Controlled only by our vision.

June 11, 2008

WHEN ARE WE?

Spy for me
Fly for me
Sing to me
Cling to me
Hear me
Fear me

The world continues to spin

Live with me
Give to me
Dance with me
Prance with me
Spin with me
Grin with me

Time has no beginning
Has no end

The world turns
Time flows
Age has no meaning
To the cosmos
We are
Or we are not

Life is but the shadow
Of eternity

6/11/08

EMOTIONALITY

Across the vastness of emotional time
Silence flows through vectors of thought
Releasing charged shafts without discretion.
Slings of netted gauze absorb most of these rays
But a few, unimpeded, speed on to their tasks,
As unbidden motes of fleeting feelings
Spiriting thoughts wholly encased within
Shards of time.
As the target of such silent attacks
One is sent reeling within a visual spectrum
Of floating orbs flashing before one's eyes,
Never really visualized but experienced nonetheless
As a warning of impending abandonment.
So as one silently lies down to dampen the effect
Leaving alertness to its own devices
By allowing a slow dawning of consciousness—
Likened to a staring into slatted eyes
Boldly gazing within inches of one's face.
Gone are the defenses as the swelling
Strips away the gauze and permits more spears
To trigger their reactions.

June 28, 2008

EMOTIONS

Emotions guide our thoughts as well as our actions.
They bring to the surface needs we don't want to know
And fill our thoughts with flights of fantasy.
We are at their mercy, traveling with them embedded
Within our actions, often hidden frequently unbidden.
They come to us as tendrils gracefully wrapped around our heart
And gently insert their will upon our thoughts.
We welcome them at first for they acknowledge
That we are alive and a part of the community of man.
Then they assert their power, ever so subtly
And disrupt our status quo.
Soon they rewrite our route through life
And cause us to act beyond our want.
Soon they will remake our image from within and without.
With experience we may keep them subdued
But never controlled.
With practice we may suppress their bidding
But never completely.
With care we may continue on our path
But never complacently.
Emotions make us who we are.
But they can unmake who we are becoming.
This can be good or bad
But never without a cost.

Nov. 28, 2008

HOW WE LIVE

Pain speaks to us as a reminder of ourselves.
It seeks deep within to draw our attention,
Be it physical or emotional.
To live with pain is to be alive
To overcome pain is to live.

Chance entangles lives with options newly brought.
To choose denies chance its power
And relegates it to the company of the ordinary.
To accept chance is to invite its randomness into our lives,
To deny us the power to decide our own paths.
Thus to be slaves to its influence.
To deny chance is to grasp the reins of life,
To determine our own fate.

Attitude is the deciding power in the world.
We often seek to dominate our environs
But not ourselves.
We deny our power for directing our course
And wind up in the pile deleted from life.
Reawaken this titan
Energize this sleeping soul
Decide how things are and how they will be in our lives
And experience the dream
So long dormant deep within us.

It is always the morning of our lives,
A dawn for us.
Let us gather our inner forces and
Grasp control from chance's dance
And guide ourselves with our determination
To meet life freely on level ground as equals.

Nov. 2008

LIFE

Stand before the sign
Salute your brethren working to set you free.
Think—
Use your brain
Brawn looks good, but fails in its time.

Misty eyes cast long shadows
Highlighting the flashes of lightning on dew.
Where among your varied parts are the forces
You pride yourself in?
Where is the power that will drive you
Beyond endurance?
Think—
Use your brain
Learn and love.
Conquer yourself—
Give in to your inner self and express it.
Give of yourself and
Be yourself.

Life is powered by love
And love empowers life.
One is the same as the other.

Nov. 2008

LIVING 2

Sliding
Slipping
Falling
Gripping
No where to go
No one to see
Life passes
And we sit
Sinking
Fleeing
Alone.

Nov. 2008

PRAYER

Silently asking for guidance and love
Not knowing whether it is heard or not,
Gathering within us the thoughts and needs,
For us and for others.
Is it selfish to request for help?
Is it hypocritical to include others?
How do we know if our prayers are really sincere?
Or is the inclusion of others so that they might be heard?

We are told prayer has power.
It can move mountains.
But can it move us?
How does one open one's heart and mind
So that they can be moved?
How can one listen for the answers
So that a change can take place?

Somewhere beyond the scope of seeing
Lays the field of knowing.
Within that field are the wisps of thoughts
Seeking the right knoll
Where fulfillment sleeps.
Not that it is not there for us to find
But it is there for us to arouse.
Nothing comes free, not even our breath.
We pay by our doing and with our care for others.

Nov. 28, 2008

FREE ASSOCIATION

Strange
I feel strange.
Never have I felt so free and tied down at one time.
My options are wide open, yet I have closed them off.
Where is my head that it flies through the air but never leaves my neck?
Where do I see the visions of peace and tranquility?
Why am I amidst a war of tornadoes?

Above cruise clouds drifting without rearranging
Yet here am I among the trees with swirling leaves.
Never have I been so tangled within the web of consciousness
Enclosed in the net of unconsciousness.
How clever the seine has been woven, even by my mind
I can never see the tail but know the end is near.
Finally the scene ends and the weird visions fade
But nowhere do I see a signpost to direct me.
Groping in the dark my talons scratch the veneer of reality
And pierce the wall enclosing my imagination.
Hang on and enjoy the ride.
Swirl and twirl through the cerebral stratosphere
Enmeshed with words of longing, yearning, hope, and certainty.

And now, where will it go?
From whence has it come?
And Why?

Dec. 1, 2008

GROWTH OF CONVICTION

Careless thoughts can wring agonizing feelings from the mind.
Careless minds can cause agonizing actions from people.
Careless people create agonizing consequences for themselves.

By careless it is meant to be without thought
To not think through one's plans or actions
Thus to ensure outcomes not wanted and poorly received.

Upon the flight of time, tracing paths across the blank slate of the mind
A nameless form slowly takes shape beckoning us to join it
A future, unnamed, unplanned, undirected, not knowing how to smile.

Reeling from the impact of this formless form
Thoughts swim in the whirlpool of confusion
Valiantly struggling to escape from its defectiveness.

Minutely crawling to appear unseen as the wisps of the mist swirl to corral it
A coherent thought emerges to address its progenitor with determined antagonism
Firmly standing against the maelstrom of conventionality to assert itself independently.

Conserving energy to propel itself forward and choosing its path carefully
Intently seeking signs of traps to its individuality
Growing strong on the convictions learned within the pale of mediocrity

Alive it strongly strides through the diminishing mists of collusion
Resisting the clinging grasps of the hands of conformity
Announcing "I Am Here" and who is to stop me?

Dec. 1, 2008

ARE WE THERE YET?

We dance before the wind of change
Holding forth on our thesis of social interaction.
Aloft the sounds of tomorrow's storms echo
In the chamber of our sensibilities.
Yesterday's dreams become today's realities if acted upon,
While sleep overtakes those who stand still.
Seeing beyond the horizons of today's knowledge
To scenes of yet to happen acts as they unfold.
Here we are, poised upon the brink of the chasm of nothingness
Searching for a hand hold, not evident nor to be found.
And yet beyond our waking world we dance to tunes
Varying with our moods, and giving off an aura of certainty.
Each step leads us further along the path
Striving to perceive the impressions gifted to us
But frustrated by the fog shrouding our brains.
Still, we press on praying for a chance to grasp the views
Offered but not presented outright.
Yes, we are here, and
No, we are not.
This is the realm of our dreams floating on waves of air.
We know this, yet are still enthralled by its veneer of reality
And its enticements.

Dec. 10, 2008

SILENCE, PERHAPS

Silenced echoes reverberate through invisible halls
Erected to contain emotions.
Where then are the portals allowing sound to circulate?
Curtained by waves of wind wafting in unfelt breezes
Undulating upon the tides of time
But silenced, stilled, silenced.

Drifting along on the currents of air
Deftly floating high above the troubled turbulence,
Seeking nowhere but encompassing everywhere.
Alone among the throngs of souls seeking peace
Grasping within the bounds of envy
And being engulfed by the silence,
Always the silence.

The mind, any mind, my mind, your mind
Emits its energies when encountering one another
As they, we sail past our life's journey posts
Imprinting our marks, often without merit.

Unbeknown to us, by us, or through us,
We blindly run our course thinking we know.
Fooling ourselves into believing we are in charge.
But truly we are asleep in our silence,
Forever the silence

With ignorance comes bliss until we are nudged,
Until we are stirred, until we pretend to awaken.
Then we bluster, at least within ourselves, or to ourselves
As we take control, lead, or go through the motions.
We scream against the follies of man
When it is our folly we are objecting to.
We strut about asserting our will,
Dragging those who would follow along,
In silence, enforced silence.

Perhaps we will awaken and really look about ourselves
Become aware of the shifts in the road ahead.
Perhaps we can grab onto one of our pillars
And attach our beings to our lost dream.
Perhaps we will truly awaken
And hear the silence from which we have emerged
As it fills our ears with harmonies vaguely remembered but there
    nonetheless.
Perhaps the dream will open us to life
So we can know who, what, and why we are.
Perhaps, perhaps.

The dream is the fuel and the compass
Formed from the silence
The introspective silence.

Sept. 3, 2009

TRAVELLER'S LAMENT

Sitting
Sitting
Sitting
Always on the go
But sitting
Sitting
Sitting

Sept. 13, 2009

LIFE'S CLOUDS

Castles rising in the sky, majestically billowing upward.
Towers of gray and white frothing about within themselves
Melding and reforming, drifting across the vast expanse of our vision
To dissipate into mists of vapor only to reform in more fantastic ways.

Our lives are like these clouds, always being buffeted by the winds of life
Being drained of substances heretofore stable but now the essence of rain.
Forcing us to reform and reconstruct our lives and thoughts
Enabling us to step over the traps, and through the mire of circumstance.

Alert to the path we take we can form our defenses and protect our cause
Skimming over the fetching fingers of fate and sailing past the reefs of failed fortunes.
New technologies afford us a pause enabling us to scan the horizon for obstacles
Cleverly designed to entrap us with promised desires and affordable futures.

Our defense is within our minds as we learn to feel our thoughts,
To reach inside and pull out the habit of repayable convenience,
To cast it among the heap of unused and discarded traditions
Designed to relegate us to similar fates of chosen comforts.

Alas, we are programmed by the same technology to "accept what is our due"
After all, we have enslaved ourselves to the systems taught in every school,
Not how to "to our own selves be true," but how to trade our dreams for comfort.
Not the comfort of our dreams, but the comfort of our means.
Breaking free of this slavery is not a task for the meek.
However, inside each of us are the means and the strength.
We need but to tap within and draw forth the energy
As we sever the ties that chain us to our posts of everyday life.

Then we can soar among the castles in our mind's eye
Reforming and reshaping our destinies with but a thought
Bringing to life the long forgotten dreams and needs
Smothered by the concerns of those who never went forth.

We are the future
We are the dream
We can do it
We will win.

Sept. 17, 2009

HOW WE BECOME WHO WE ARE

A single tear lingers at the brink
Hesitating, considering its course,
Knowing that it will open the flow
Or contain the flood.

A single drops flows within the river of time
Commanding attention by subtly grabbing the stage,
Announcing its presence through refracting light
And leaving intangible footprints in the march of time.

We rise above the crowd by our thoughts,
We hide among the throngs with our silence,
We lead with our abilities trained for us,
We follow, hoping not to be noticed.

After we face ourselves, we hesitate
Considering our course
Knowing that when we take that step
We are committed.

We stand looking upon the universal fields
Straining to feel the grass between our toes,
Yearning to have the breezes caress our skin,
Sighing from deep within—contentedly.
As we go forth in life and experience what it has to offer,
We dwell on those things we deem most important.
But how do we pick them?
From which warehouse of stored information do we pick?
Here are some we love, here some we like, here some we hate.

Which become our guiding lights?
Which determined our self?
Which makes our decisions?
Is being conscious of our choices really a prime factor?

Alone at night with only ourselves to deal with
Who can we really fool?
What face can we put on?
Does it really matter to our mind knowing it never forgets?
Try as we might, we cannot blind our mind's eye.
It sees through our facades and is not fooled by our charades.
When we accept that we are human and thus not perfect,
When we accept that there is no one who is faultless,
When we accept that we succeed in spite of our shortcomings,
When we accept that our attitude is paramount,
Then we accept who and what we are, and can grow through life,
Then the single tear knows what it must do,
Then we are living by our own choices, be they good or bad,
Then we can be guided through the maze to new insights
And merge who we are with who we can be.

Sept. 23, 2009

SAGE OR SENIOR

As years pass
And lines define our visage
Wisdom fills in the cracks.
But are we open to this?
Do we really allow
Knowledge
To insidiously seep in?
At what point do we go
From Senior to Sage?

All of us have his store of experiences.
Some of us have learned from them.
This veritable mass of information can be
Readily available to guide and teach.
But society seems to dismiss us as outmoded,
Not relevant in this web culture,
Not informative in this Age of Information.
We are seen as dated,
Only applicable to time and place
A source for historical comparison,
Not relevant in this modern age.

In this you err grievously!
Of course times have changed
Of course the world has progressed
Of course technology has grown
But people, yes people, are the same.
Humans react as they always have
Love, hate, fear still are found within,
Stress, anxiety, depression abound.
We are your resource
The repository of human experience.
Deny this and limit your potential.
All progress is built upon the past
Great men stand above the masses
By standing upon the shoulders of giants.
We, your discarded masses,
Your forgotten sources,
Are the foundations of the future
And the comforts of the past.

Jan. 7, 2010

TODAY'S CHAOS

Standing amid this chaos
Staring at the organized disorganization
Silently screaming for someone—anyone
To acknowledge this insanity
Feeling frustrated, betrayed, disappointed
Knowing silence cannot be heard.

Who am I to rant, to rail?
Who am I indeed to be self-righteous?
I, who sees the pattern in this chaos
Am quietly standing,
Am quietly bemoaning
A fate I have helped to create
By my silence!

We who claim to have foresight
Or at least to see the path
Ought not stand aside and tacitly complain
Bemoan our fate in silence.
We cannot be among the silent majority
Who claim clairvoyance.
Stand aside?
Nay!
Raise our flags, shout our claims
Heed not the darts cast by those who would profit
The missiles cast by pragmatists who see only
Their reflection in their mirror.
For change we may endure,
Heeded or not we can stand tall
For not being silent is a call to arms.

Jan. 8, 2010

EXPEDIENCY OR RESPONSIBILITY

I am here
Standing among the ruins
Of yesterday's time.
Pacing back and forth
Stepping through and over debris
Left for the future to ponder
The questions about today's
Commitment to our survival.
Where are we going?
What are we doing?
What are we thinking?
Our actions reflect our thought
Or the lack thereof.

Tomorrow's men
Digging into their past
Will have clues of us today.
Historical documents will give
Them direction
But physical debris will convince them
Of whom we really are.

It is our nature to look to our comforts
To know what is best for us.
To be sure we are right.
And for the moment it is right.
But expediency is always convenient
To those who are complacent
Not to those who are responsible.

Step out of the box,
Cast your fate with your children,
Be a guide to your lost kin,
Be an example for the future,
Not an item of the past.
We have it within our time to win
Not just for us
But for all mankind.

Jan. 12, 2010

IMMORTALITY

The past is today
As today is tomorrow.
When we are is but a point in time
Never really here but forever there.
We ride the waves of time
Thinking we are its masters
But really we are its pawns
Playing upon its playground of the moment.
We seek recognition, fame, immortality
By outrageous routes,
Never seeing the obvious,
Which is to help others.
Stardom seldom outlives its fans,
But kindness is oft remembered.
And if it is not,
Its effects are.

Jan. 12, 2010

MOULD OR NOT

Sleeping through the daylight hours
Shuts off our sense of time
And delays our need for closure.
Conscious of currents and noises
Reflects an awareness of existence
Etched within the mind.
Rising above our station
Denies a position of life
But opens the world to us.

Listen to the elders for they know about life
Follow their advice and avoid life's strife
Be what you are seen as
For this ensures ease.
Listen to the elders in order to appease.

But NO!
Step out, be who you are meant to be
Become all that is in you
And fly.
Fly beyond your mould,
Resist the the enticing ease.

Life offers a blank page
Neither printed nor written upon
Only you have the pen
To mark it at will
But you need to do it
If your life, you will fulfill.

Others will rail at your rebellion
Seeing your path as absurd,
But within your heart lies the fire
To help you rise higher
And avoid the common quagmire.

We have a choice given freely
Our hand can direct our way
If we but stand upon our ground
Determined to have our say.

Jan. 13, 2010

www.ingramcontent.com/pod-product-compliance
Ingram Content Group UK Ltd.
Pitfield, Milton Keynes, MK11 3LW, UK
UKHW041953230426
12048UKWH00008B/318